MW01140094

WOMEN'S SOCCER
ON THE RISE

WOMEN'S SOCCER TODAY

Superstars of Women's Soccer

Top Teams in Women's Soccer

U.S. Women's Team

Women's Soccer on the Rise

WOMEN'S SOCCER
ON THE RISE

ELIZABETH ROSEBOROUGH

MASON CREST

Mason Crest
450 Parkway Drive, Suite D
Broomall, Pennsylvania 19008
(866) MCP-BOOK (toll free)

First printing
9 8 7 6 5 4 3 2 1

ISBN (hardback) 978-1-4222-4216-2
ISBN (series) 978-1-4222-4212-4
ISBN (ebook) 978-1-4222-7598-6

Library of Congress Cataloging-in-Publication Data on file

Developed and Produced by National Highlights Inc.
Editor: Andrew Luke
Interior and cover design: Annalisa Gumbrecht, Studio Gumbrecht
Production: Michelle Luke

QR CODES AND LINKS TO THIRD-PARTY CONTENT

CONTENTS

Chapter 1 Growing Strong.. 7

Chapter 2 College Soccer.. 21

Chapter 3 Going Pro... 35

Chapter 4 Playing Fair.. 51

Chapter 5 Changes at the Top.. 65

            Glossary of Soccer Terms................................... 76

            Further Reading, Internet Resources........................ 77

            Index.. 78

            Author's Biography and Credits............................. 80

KEY ICONS TO LOOK FOR:

 WORDS TO UNDERSTAND: These words with their easy-to-understand definitions will increase the reader's understanding of the text while building vocabulary skills.

 SIDEBARS: This boxed material within the main text allows readers to build knowledge, gain insights, explore possibilities, and broaden their perspectives by weaving together additional information to provide realistic and holistic perspectives.

 EDUCATIONAL VIDEOS: Readers can view videos by scanning our QR codes, providing them with additional educational content to supplement the text. Examples include news coverage, moments in history, speeches, iconic sports moments, and much more!

 TEXT-DEPENDENT QUESTIONS: These questions send the reader back to the text for more careful attention to the evidence presented there.

 RESEARCH PROJECTS: Readers are pointed toward areas of further inquiry connected to each chapter. Suggestions are provided for projects that encourage deeper research and analysis.

WORDS TO UNDERSTAND

AYSO
(American Youth Soccer Organization) a national organization for the sport in the United States for children ages four through nineteen

era
a long, distinct period of time in history

FIFA
Fédération Internationale de Football Association, or in English, International Federation of Association Football; the governing body for soccer on the international level

CHAPTER 1

Growing Strong

Girls across the world love lacing up their cleats and heading out to the soccer field to play the beautiful game. We'll take a look at how far women's soccer has come, how girls' soccer is growing in the United States, why sports are so important for the well-being of girls, and why the U.S. Women's Soccer Team is viewed across the world as the gold standard for women's soccer. Women's soccer is growing fast—do your best to keep up!

YOUTH SOCCER: FROM THE BEGINNING

Every weekend, across continents all over the world, thousands of girls hit the soccer field. Sometimes, girls simply get together with friends to play an informal game, while other girls enjoy playing competitively. While this is the norm now, it hasn't always been this way. Women have casually played soccer for a very, very long time, but it has taken many years for female soccer players to have the opportunity to become professional paid athletes. Many people say that women have not been interested in sports for a very long time, but that simply could not be further from the truth. There is evidence of women enjoying the sport as early as 1869. There were pictures featured in the popular magazine *Harper's Bazaar* of women kicking the ball around and enjoying a casual game. It's extremely likely that women played soccer together before this, even though it wasn't recorded or captured on film. In the late 1800s, women began to play organized games similar to men's games.

These games had referees and scorekeepers and were regarded as a form of entertainment for the community. Some of the women's matches attracted as many as ten thousand fans. While this may not seem like a lot when we think about how many people today's giant stadiums hold, this was an incredible number of fans in one place during this era, especially for a women's event.

Girls around the world, like these schoolgirls in England, have played soccer in one form or another since the turn of last century.

A TURN FOR THE WORSE

According to BBC News, in the 1920s many in the sport's hierarchy believed women's soccer was growing too popular—to the point that women's soccer may have been on its way to becoming more popular than men's soccer. For a time, professional soccer organizations actually suggested that men's clubs should refuse to allow women's teams to use their facilities. Basically, these professional organizations were attempting to put a ban on women's soccer. While not all national organizations put these rules into place, many did. In most countries, organized women's soccer simply ceased to exist.

Women still played on their own, but since they were banned from professional facilities, they were unable to hold official practices and games. This made it difficult for teams to get organized and play against one another. Eventually the bans were lifted, but it took nearly fifty years for women's soccer to begin to gain popularity once again.

KICKING THINGS BACK UP

In the 1960s soccer began to gain some popularity in the United States, where it had long failed to appeal to American audiences. This newfound popularity was especially notable among children and is attributed to the prominence of college soccer and the emergence of the first professional soccer leagues. The National Professional Soccer League (NPSL), an American league launched by a group of wealthy entrepreneurs in 1967, even had a national television contract with broadcaster CBS. The NPSL merged into the North American Soccer League (NASL) the next year, a league that helped the popularity of the sport surge. In 1964, **AYSO** was developed in California in an effort to bring soccer to young children in a low-pressure, fun environment. This was an alternative to school sports, which often were only for older children and involved cutting less-skilled children from the team. While AYSO was a great idea, in the beginning it only allowed boys to play soccer. Many girls were interested in playing, but there simply wasn't a place for them to get involved. Girls were so excited about soccer that many of them began asking to play on boys' teams. Some boys' teams welcomed girls, but most did not. Girls found themselves interested in soccer with nowhere to play in an organized setting.

Even after AYSO was established in 1964, there was no organized way for girls to practice and play soccer.

GIRL POWER!

In 1971, three California soccer coaches—Joe Korbus, Mario Maehabo, and Ron Rickleffs—decided to create an AYSO team just for girls, and the rest is history. Today, 40 percent of AYSO athletes are girls. While AYSO is the most recognizable name in youth soccer, there are a variety of different organizations that provide soccer coaching to young girls. Programs like Lil' Kickers and Soccer Shots provide soccer instruction and experience to pre-kindergarten and elementary-school-age boys and girls. These programs focus on building teamwork, agility, and conditioning skills while also teaching children how to play the game. One of the goals of these programs is to ensure that kids are learning that sports and exercise are fun. U.S. Youth Soccer is an organization similar to AYSO that helps millions of children learn the game each year. U.S. Youth Soccer has some leagues that are quite competitive. These leagues work to help children get college scholarships or work toward becoming professional soccer players.

OPEN REGISTRATION VS. CUTS

One of the key factors in many soccer programs for young children is open registration. This means that all children who want to play are assigned to a team, and they do not have to worry about being cut. Some youth soccer programs do require tryouts, but the purpose of these tryouts is simply to ensure that teams are balanced—meaning that one team does not end up with a lot of highly skilled players while another team ends up with a lot of beginner-level players. Youth soccer teams typically focus on helping kids learn the game rather than being ultra competitive. If children do become highly skilled, they often leave open-registration teams and begin playing with a more competitive soccer club. Club soccer typically involves some travel and is more expensive to play than open-registration soccer. If you're just starting to hone your soccer skills, it's a good idea to start with an open-registration team. This will ensure that you get plenty of playing and practice time to improve your skills and conditioning before you try out for a more competitive club team.

Open-registration leagues are a good place for girls to play and improve before trying to make more competitive club teams.

GAINING MOMENTUM

Over the past twenty-five years, girls' soccer in the United States has gained unstoppable momentum. In the 1980s and early 1990s, soccer wasn't talked about much in the United States. It was viewed as a European game and most people in the United States did not play or follow the sport. Some people viewed soccer the way that many people today view polo or rugby—a foreign sport for people who have lots of money. While soccer does not require much equipment, many people felt that soccer was an exclusive sport for people who had the money for private clubs and expensive coaching. In many areas of the United States, soccer clubs required joining fees and extensive travel to tournaments. This monetary requirement made it quite difficult for many lower-income children to play. While it has always been easy for children to kick the ball around, playing in an "official" capacity had often been reserved for kids from privileged backgrounds.

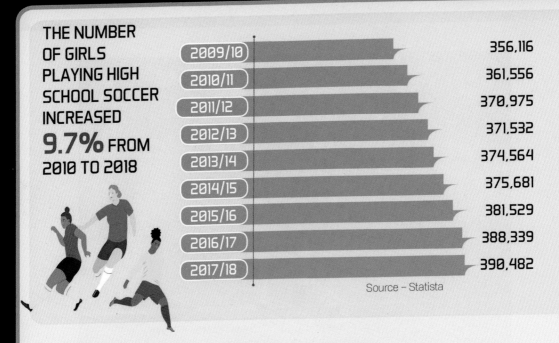

THE NUMBER OF GIRLS PLAYING HIGH SCHOOL SOCCER INCREASED

9.7% FROM 2010 TO 2018

Year	Number
2009/10	356,116
2010/11	361,556
2011/12	370,975
2012/13	371,532
2013/14	374,564
2014/15	375,681
2015/16	381,529
2016/17	388,339
2017/18	390,482

Source – Statista

The United States and Canada account for almost half of the 4.8 million female players registered at worldwide level in 2014. UEFA member associations also play a significant role by representing 44% of all registered female players. In terms of participation, women's soccer is still heavily under-developed in the remaining associations and confederations.

2,255,000

2,095,803

CONCACAF

UEFA

AFC

2,287,285

CAF

300,122

CONMEBOL

54,055

25,459

OFC

38,736

Source – FIFA

Senior players represent a minority of registered female players, at 46% overall. This holds true in all confederations except for CONMEBOL and CONCACAF (excluding the United States and Canada). This shows the necessity for these Confederations to put more emphasis on youth development (under 17 years of age) of the women's game.

CONFEDERATION/JUNIOR/SENIOR

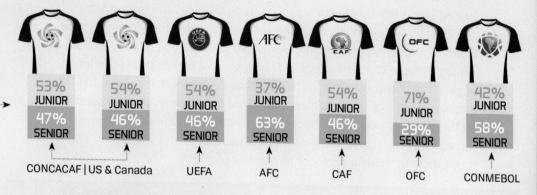

53% JUNIOR	54% JUNIOR	54% JUNIOR	37% JUNIOR	54% JUNIOR	71% JUNIOR	42% JUNIOR
47% SENIOR	46% SENIOR	46% SENIOR	63% SENIOR	46% SENIOR	29% SENIOR	58% SENIOR
CONCACAF | US & Canada		UEFA	AFC	CAF	OFC	CONMEBOL

4TH

IN 2017, SOCCER WAS THE MOST POPULAR HIGH SCHOOL SPORT FOR GIRLS

TRACK & FIELD	494,477
VOLLEYBALL	444,779
BASKETBALL	430,368
SOCCER	**388,339**
SOFTBALL	367,405
CROSS COUNTRY	226,039
SWIMMING & DIVING	170,797
TENNIS	158,171
COMPETITIVE SPIRIT	144,243
LACROSSE	93,473

Source – NFHS

13

PARTICIPATION RATES

Thirty percent of households in the United States have at least one family member who plays soccer. The number of girls who play soccer in the United States has slowly but surely been on the rise. The United States currently has more children playing soccer than any other country in the world. Approximately 3.9 million American children play soccer, and 1.6 million of those children are girls. This number is higher than the number of girls that play soccer in all other countries combined. It's likely that the massive success of the U.S. Women's World Cup team is partly responsible for this amazing popularity. Soccer is currently the number three most-played sport by high school girls (behind basketball and volleyball), and is slowly inching closer and closer to number one.

The tremendous success of the USWNT is largely responsible for the explosion in popularity of girls' soccer.

Girls in Sports: Why It Matters

It's hard to imagine now, but many years ago it was rare for girls to participate in organized sports. Girls and women were encouraged to work in the home, and it was frowned upon for them to exert themselves with recreational activity. Luckily, that has changed in the United States over the past seventy-five years. There are a number of reasons that girls benefit from playing sports. Girls who play sports report that they feel healthier than girls who do not play sports. They don't get sick as often, and they have reduced rates of cigarette and drug use. Mentally, the benefits are myriad—girls who play sports tend to get better grades in school, have higher self-confidence, have lower rates of depression and suicide, and have stronger relationships within their communities. Girls who play sports also report that they have stronger friendships, and they feel that they are well liked by their peers.

GAINING EXPOSURE THROUGH THE WORLD CUP

While many Americans follow soccer today, this was not always the case, especially prior to the 1990s. Americans saw soccer (known as football in most of the rest of the world) as slow and low scoring when compared to American football, basketball, and baseball. In 1994, a huge shift occurred when the United States got the opportunity to host the men's FIFA World Cup Finals. Since the North American Soccer League folded in 1984, Americans were able to watch professional soccer matches only on television, as the only pro leagues were in other countries. When the World Cup was hosted by the United States, Americans were able

Major League Soccer began play in 1996 after the surge in popularity of the sport caused by hosting the 1994 men's FIFA World Cup in the United States. The spotlight continued to be on the men's game rather than the women's.

to attend the matches in person. Soccer was everywhere, and the United States fell in love with the passionate, fast-paced, beautiful game. The 1994 World Cup received unprecedented TV ratings for the sport in America. Americans became enamored with soccer. A new pro league, Major League Soccer (MLS), started play in 1996. Sign-ups for children's soccer went through the roof as kids began to look up to the professional soccer athletes they saw on TV. Many youth soccer programs had to add additional teams to accommodate all of the new sign-ups. Adults and children alike marveled at watching some of the best athletes in the world on the soccer field. At the time, most Americans were more interested in men's soccer than women's soccer, but that was all about to change.

1999: THE BIG WIN

America's interest in women's soccer blew up when the 1999 U.S. Women's Soccer Team won the FIFA Women's World Cup. Their victory was as celebrated as gold medals at the Olympics. Professional women's soccer was rarely watched or discussed in the United States prior to this point. Suddenly, young girls all over the United States wanted to be just like soccer superstars Mia Hamm and Brandi Chastain. Up until that point, girls' soccer teams existed, but they were not given nearly as much attention as boy's teams. The World Cup win inspired many competitive soccer clubs (and youth clubs) to dedicate more time and training to their girls' teams. Many girls realized that with hard work and dedication they too could become professional soccer athletes. This led many girls to want to learn more about how they could start playing competitively.

GIVING BACK TO GIRLS

The USWNT is the beacon for women's soccer in all countries around the world where women strive to be respected as soccer players.

While soccer is not as expensive as some other sports, there are many neighborhoods both in the United States and across the world that do not have the resources or the facilities necessary to accommodate youth soccer programs. Programs such as Goals for Girls help bring soccer to girls all over the world, helping young female athletes to grow their athletic skills while also increasing their self-esteem. Goals for Girls matches an American-based soccer team with former or current professional women's soccer players, and together they conduct soccer clinics in other countries. Goals for Girls also has U. S.-based programs in which they conduct clinics and provide equipment to girls who may not otherwise have such opportunities. Programs like Goals for Girls are one of the many ways that professional athletes give back to the communities around them.

THE GOLD STANDARD: U.S. WOMEN'S NATIONAL TEAM

All over the world, women's soccer teams look to the United States team (USWNT) as the example that they want to emulate. There are a few reasons for this. First, the women on the team are incredible athletes who are difficult to beat. They have three World Cup championships and four Olympic gold medals. Secondly, the USWNT is not treated

as a second-rate version of the men's team. They have their own training, coaches, and facilities. While the United States still has a long way to go in terms of gender equality in the sport, it is far ahead of much of the rest of the world in this matter. Women's soccer teams in many other countries strive for the recognition and respect that the USWNT receives.

Former USWNT star Mia Hamm is one of the most recognizable names in professional women's soccer. Check out some of her career highlights here!

In some parts of the world women are not seen as serious athletes, no matter how accomplished they are or how hard they train. It can be difficult for these women to find proper training and coaching, especially in cultures where they are expected to be the primary caretaker of their families, making it challenging to fully dedicate themselves to their sport. Some of

these countries are making progress toward equal treatment of male and female athletes. Many of these athletes look to the United States as the gold standard of how women should be treated in athletics.

All-time USWNT goal scorer Abby Wamback poses with girls at a soccer clinic in Japan. USWNT members give back to the soccer community around the world to help bring the game to areas where it needs support.

Many members of the USWNT make a point to give back to their communities, and teams across the world respect this pay-it-forward nature. From working with organizations that bring soccer to girls in low-income communities to appearing at charitable events, these professional athletes can be counted on to give back.

TEXT-DEPENDENT QUESTIONS:

1. In what year did AYSO begin to allow girls to play soccer?

2. What percentage of households in the United States have at least one family member that plays soccer?

3. What's the difference between soccer organizations that allow open registration and those that do not?

RESEARCH PROJECT:

The USWNT is the gold standard that other countries attempt to model their women's soccer programs after. Choose two other countries and compare and contrast their women's soccer programs to women's soccer in the United States. What are the similarities? What are the differences? Highlight three of each.

WORDS TO UNDERSTAND

formidable
having qualities that discourage approach or attack

NCAA
National Collegiate Athletic Association; a non-profit regulatory organization in the United States that creates and enforces rules and regulations for athletics in both public and private institutions of higher education

revenue
the total income produced by a given source

CHAPTER 2

College Soccer

Can you imagine a world in which girls and women do not have the same opportunity to play sports as boys and men? Not long ago, this was a reality in the United States. Imagine: boys and men are supported, coached, and given opportunities to develop their athletic talents, while girls and women have no choice but to watch from the sidelines. While this is hard to picture in this day and age, sixty years ago this was status quo for many girls and women throughout the United States. Over time, people who felt passionately that both men and women should have equal opportunities to play sports have taken action and leveled the playing field.

NCAA DIVISION I WOMEN'S SOCCER: THE BEGINNING

Castleton State College in Vermont was the site of the nation's first collegiate women's varsity team.

Today, colleges and universities have amazing women's soccer programs with top-level training and highly regarded coaches, and in many cases, these programs were a fairly recent development. For years, colleges only had men's soccer programs and often did not even have a club team for women who were interested in the sport. Thankfully, things have changed in a big way.

The first collegiate women's varsity soccer team was founded at Castleton State College in Castleton, VT in 1966. Prior to the formation of this team women's soccer existed at the school, but it was purely in the form of a club sport. This meant that the women's team did not receive funding or get to participate at the same level of competition as the men's varsity-level team. Basically, women's collegiate soccer was seen as a hobby for the players, while men's varsity soccer was viewed as a real sport, with the potential for players to eventually play at the professional level. Playing professionally was not even in the realm of possibility for women at the time, as women's professional soccer did not exist in the United States. The women on the club team at Castleton organized their own practices, coordinated their own training, organized their own game schedule, and paid for their own equipment.

This was not just the case at Castleton—most women's soccer clubs across the country were in the same boat. After Castleton created its own women's varsity soccer program, some other schools (including the University of North Carolina at Chapel Hill, or UNC) began to follow suit. As women's soccer began to be taken more seriously at the college level, it started to gain popularity with younger girls in high school. Many girls who enjoyed soccer began to consider the possibility of an athletic scholarship to help them pay for college. In the mid-1960s soccer became more popular in gym classes throughout the United States, as it was seen as a relatively inexpensive way for students to get exercise with a lower rate of injury than other sports, such as softball or basketball. Development of soccer at the high-school level was key for creating players who would eventually excel at the collegiate level.

While women's soccer began to be recognized as a legitimate collegiate varsity sport in the 1960s, funding left much to be desired on many women's soccer teams. In comparison to men's collegiate soccer teams, women's teams typically had less-experienced coaches (who received lower salaries than the men's coaches), older facilities, less money for travel and equipment, less money for recruiting players, and less money available to athletes in the form of scholarships. In order to succeed, women had to figure out how to do more with less. In the 1970s, a huge step was taken for equality in women's sports with the passing of the Education Amendments of 1972. This included Title IX, which stated that schools receiving any amount of public funding had to give equal access and funding to both male and female sports.

Equal meant that if a school had a boy's soccer team, they needed to offer the sport to girls as well. In the case where sports do not have a female equivalent (such as American football), girls are legally required to be given the opportunity to play if they choose to do so. If the school holds tryouts, female student-athletes must be able to perform at the same level as male student-athletes in order to participate. With this law in place, many schools that previously had only club soccer teams for women began to establish varsity teams to create an equal playing field for both men and women. This law affected schools all the way down to the elementary-school level.

The Title IX Act impacted female sports all the way down to the elementary-school level.

After Title IX was established, colleges began to see what female athletes could do with proper facilities, coaching, and training. Women already had the drive they needed to succeed in athletics, and with the advent of Title IX they finally had the proper tools to take them to the next level. Colleges began to recruit promising female student-athletes and provide athletic scholarships to them. In 1974, Ann Meyers committed to playing basketball at UCLA and became the first female student-athlete to receive a full scholarship. High school girl soccer players began to take athletics more seriously as they realized that being a star player could be a ticket to getting a college scholarship. The growth of women's soccer took some time, but by 1981 there were approximately one hundred varsity women's collegiate soccer programs throughout the United States.

It wasn't until 1982 that the NCAA began to sponsor women's teams. While today this seems like an obvious move, it upset many people in the college-sports world at the time. Although it's hard to imagine, some college athletics fans and leaders still had the long-held belief that sports were for men, and money should not be spent to give women the same athletic opportunities as their male counterparts. Regardless, the NCAA held strong and continued to sponsor and support women's collegiate athletics. Women's soccer quickly became more popular in the world of college sports. It did not simply begin in one area of the country, as is the history of men's college soccer, which grew primarily in the Northeast. As funding became available (and required by law), women's soccer programs grew evenly throughout the colleges and universities of the United States. This was important to the growth of the game because it allowed varsity women's teams to have other teams to play without requiring extensive (and costly) travel. Today, more colleges and universities sponsor women's soccer (1,040 schools) than sponsor men's soccer (838 schools). This is just one of the testaments to how quickly women's soccer has flourished in the United States. The incredible growth of collegiate women's soccer paved the way for professional women's soccer to take hold.

Australia's Sam Kerr is one of the most prolific goal scorers in the women's game. She is the leading career goal scorer in the NWSL.

DIVISION I: ONLY THE BEST

While women's college soccer rose evenly across the country in the 1980s, some schools had programs that stood out more than others—specifically, Division I schools. Among student-athletes, Division I schools are the most sought-after colleges and universities. Typically, Division I schools have the largest student bodies, the largest athletic department budgets, and the largest amount of scholarship money set aside for student-athletes. These schools are often celebrated more for their athletic programs than for their academics, and their sports bring in a large amount of revenue to the school. Many student-athletes enjoy playing sports at these schools because of the huge fan bases and extensive community support for athletics.

Players at Division I schools, like these players from Utah and Arizona State, are looking for programs with top-notch coaching and facilities.

Some Division I schools include Duke University, Penn State University, and the University of North Carolina at Chapel Hill. There are almost 350 schools nationwide that fall into the Division I category, and many of them are standouts in women's soccer, men's soccer, or both. At these schools there are more than six thousand Division I athletic teams, allowing more than 170,000 student-athletes to compete in collegiate sports each academic year. Division I schools provide a tremendous opportunity to student-athletes who are interested in gaining increased visibility to professional programs. Professional scouts regularly attend Division I athletic competitions.

Getting into a Division I school on an athletic scholarship is tough—they accept only the best of the best. While one out of every thirteen girls who play soccer in high school will go on to play in some capacity in college, only one out of every eighty-seven girls who play in high school will go on to play at a Division I school. After that, the competition gets even more stiff—only one out of every 835 girls will end up with a professional women's soccer contract after college.

Division I schools tend to attract the most serious high school student-athletes because their higher athletics budgets often mean that they have better facilities and better coaching. This is especially important for student-athletes who are considering becoming professional athletes after they graduate. Division I schools also have more money to spend on recruiting, which means that they are able to spend more time and resources attracting the biggest names in high school sports to their schools. When high school athletes are looking for a college where they will be challenged by playing against the best athletes in the game, Division I is the only way to go. While Division I schools have a larger amount of resources, they also have higher expectations of their student-athletes than do Division II and Division III schools.

Many Division I schools are difficult to get into (in both the areas of academics and athletics), because they are sought after by student-athletes more than schools in other divisions. The NCAA sets minimum academic requirements for athletes to maintain a scholarship, but the difficulty of meeting these requirements varies from school to school. Many Division I schools have mandatory study hours for their student-athletes. Some schools even separate their athletes from the rest of the student body so that they live, eat, practice, and sleep as a team. Being a Division I student-athlete is challenging but incredibly rewarding. A typical day for a women's soccer player can be jam-packed—practice in the morning, classes all day, homework and study hours, and classes in the evening. In sports such as football, basketball, and soccer almost all athletes who play at a professional level were once student-athletes at Division I schools.

When considering a Division I school, it's important for an athlete to think about the cost of her education. There is technically no such thing as a full-ride scholarship for Division I women's soccer, or any other women's sport outside of volleyball, tennis, gymnastics, and basketball. Athletic scholarships are awarded to many women, but they are often only partial scholarships, meaning that they will cover the cost of a portion of tuition and room and board. Scholarships are renewed on a year-to-year basis, at the coach's discretion. This means that if a player's performance or academics are not up to par, the coach can choose not to award the scholarship. This can also happen if funding is pulled or reduced.

It's rare that a scholarship will completely cover a student's tuition, and there are other factors to consider as well, including food, books, room and board, and general living expenses. Sometimes athletes take out federal loans, private loans, or both in order to subsidize the cost of living

Student-athletes must balance their training and classwork to maintain their academic standing.

during their college years. Some student-athletes also participate in work-study programs while enrolled at school. These programs allow student-athletes to work and use their paychecks toward their educational costs. While being a soccer player at a Division I school can be difficult, it can also be an incredible launchpad into a professional career. However, less than 1 percent of Division I college athletes ever receive a professional contract. This is why it's so important for student-athletes to take their academics as seriously as they do their athletics, and why schools have strict requirements that their student-athletes maintain a minimum academic standard in order to play.

Division I: How to Get There

If you're an aspiring soccer player, it makes sense that you have your sights set on one day playing for a Division I school. These schools have minimum academic requirements, so it's important that you work with your college advisor to ensure that those requirements are met. While it's essential to keep your grade point average high, it's also necessary to make sure you are taking the courses required for admission to your desired school. A strong academic and athletic foundation as early as ninth grade can help ensure that you're doing everything you can to work toward a soccer career at your dream Division I college or university. It's never too early to start working toward your goal. In fact, it may be wise to be at the top of your game even earlier than high school—some colleges and universities begin building files on potential athletes as early as seventh grade. If you aren't ready for Division I athletics straight out of high school, don't worry. Many student-athletes start at a Division II or III school and transfer to a Division I school as their skills improve.

Even students in countries known for their robust soccer programs, such as the UK, are beginning to see the value of playing soccer at a Division I school in the United States. Scholarships are offered to international students just like they are offered to U.S. students. In recent years, companies that connect foreign soccer players with U.S. universities have become a helpful tool for students interested in studying stateside. Foreign students (or their families) pay these companies a fee, and the company then connects the student with recruiters and coaches in the United States with the goal of finding a place for them on a college team.

UNIVERSITY OF NORTH CAROLINA WOMEN'S SOCCER—RUNNING THE GAME

When it comes to dominating the soccer field, there's no question that the University of North Carolina Tar Heels women's team has come out on top year after year. From their ability to recruit players who eventually become professional stars to their impressive record of championship wins,

The McCaskill Soccer Center at the University of North Carolina at Chapel Hill is home to the most successful women's soccer program in NCAA history.

the UNC Tar Heels women's soccer program is regarded by many soccer enthusiasts as the best in the United States. The Tar Heels have won twenty-two of thirty-six NCAA Division I Women's Soccer Championships and twenty of the twenty-seven Atlantic Coast Conference (ACC) Championships. While the Tar Heels are very tough to beat today, the team had humble beginnings. UNC women's soccer actually began as a club team organized by a group of women who were interested in playing but did not have a varsity team to join. In 1977, these women petitioned the school's athletic director to establish women's soccer as an official UNC varsity sport.

While it seems like the transition from club sport to varsity sport should have been a simple one, it actually took the input of many people who were well-respected decision makers in the athletic department at UNC to create the change. First, the UNC athletic director, Bill Cobey, talked with the men's soccer coach, Anson Dorrance. Cobey asked Dorrance to evaluate the women's club team and help him to decide if the players were ready to compete at the varsity level. Dorrance told Cobey that he believed the women's club team could perform well as a varsity team. Cobey then hired Dorrance as the women's coach, with the club coach, Mike Byers, as his assistant. Dorrance, who continued coaching the men's team, and Byers worked together to help mold the women's club into a full-fledged varsity team. Their first official season as a varsity team was played in 1978, but their schedule still remained a typical club schedule. Sometimes they even played high school teams, as there were not many other collegiate-level varsity women's soccer teams.

The team went through some growing pains in its first year. While this was a varsity team by name, it was not treated as such by the university. The players did, however, earn the respect of their coach. Dorrance said of the team, "These were the true pioneers. They were given nothing. They were accustomed to taking things and so they weren't as genteel as the sort of young ladies we can recruit now. They were the sort of girls who would go downtown, burn it to the ground. But then, they were on time for every single practice and in practice, they worked themselves until they were bleeding and throwing up. They had a tremendous commitment to victory and to personal athletic excellence. And for that I admired them because they were a tremendous group."

In 1979, the Association for Intercollegiate Athletics for Women (AIAW) established a national collegiate women's soccer program. With the AIAW's support, collegiate women's soccer programs began popping up all over the United States. This finally gave the UNC women's team the opportunity to play against teams that had a similar skill level. Even though many other teams were quickly established, UNC still remained the most respected, well-trained team. This was primarily because their structure had been long standing, even before their official varsity status was granted.

In 1981, the dominance of the UNC women's team truly began to shine as they continued to prove that their talent was on a different level than other, newly created varsity teams. That year UNC had the only varsity

Anson Dorrance built the UNC women's program into the most powerful force in NCAA soccer in his forty years as coach.

women's soccer team in the Southeastern United States, and Dorrance was able to leverage this to recruit one of the most talented freshman classes that the world of collegiate women's soccer has ever seen, even to this day. Dorrance had quite the advantage—girls who loved soccer and grew up in the Southeast knew that UNC was the ultimate collegiate soccer destination. Eight of these freshman recruits ended up playing as starters for the UNC team, a feat unusual for a freshman to accomplish. This class went on to help the UNC Tar Heels dominate the women's collegiate soccer circuit over the next four years. The only AIAW women's soccer championship was held in 1981, and the Tar Heels won.

As the NCAA began to sponsor collegiate women's athletics, women's championship soccer tournaments were established. The Tar Heels built on their AIAW win and went on to win the NCAA's first three women's soccer championships in 1982, 1983, and 1984. Since 1985, the Tar Heels have won eighteen NCAA championships. The Atlantic Coast Conference began holding women's soccer championships in 1987, and the Tar Heels have since won twenty-one times. While other schools do challenge the Tar Heels for dominance in women's soccer (Stanford is regarded as the latest up-and-comer), UNC has proven time and time again that they will quickly return to the first-place position.

A brief look at the commitment to conditioning of the UNC women's soccer team.

While the Tar Heels are clearly a **formidable** team as a whole, they also create powerhouse individual players. There are likely a few different factors that contribute to the creation of such amazing players, including spectacular coaching, motivation and inspiration to keep up with UNC's winning tradition, and connection with alumni who have made it to

Several current pros like Meghan Klingenberg graduated from UNC with championship pedigree.

the professional level. The most well-known athlete to graduate from the Tar Heels women's soccer program is two-time Olympic gold medalist and two-time World Cup winner Mia Hamm.

Hamm also won the FIFA Women's World Player of the Year award twice during her professional soccer career. Hamm was (and in her retirement continues to be) an advocate for the importance of getting girls active in sports. While Hamm's name is the most recognizable, there are plenty of other UNC alumni who have made names for themselves in the professional soccer world, including Tisha Venturini (gold medalist in the 1996 Olympics and member of the World Cup champion 1999 U.S. Women's National Soccer Team), Kristine Lilly (two-time Olympic gold medalist, two-time World Cup champion, most caps of any player in the history of the sport), Cindy Parlow (gold medalist in the 1996 and 2004 Olympics, member of the World Cup champion 1999 U.S. Women's National Soccer Team), Tobin Heath (gold medalist in the 2008 and 2012 Olympics, member of the World Cup champion 2015 U.S. Women's National Soccer Team), and many more.

TEXT-DEPENDENT QUESTIONS:

1. The first collegiate women's varsity soccer team was founded in 1966. At what university did this happen?

2. How many times has the UNC Tar Heels won the Atlantic Coast Conference?

3. Name three notable players who went on to play professional soccer after playing for UNC.

RESEARCH PROJECT:

While UNC has an impressive record of championship wins, Stanford and UCLA are up-and-coming powerhouses. Choose one of these two teams, and research the coaching and conditioning that these teams do to set them apart from the rest. Based on your research, explain whether you believe that the school you chose could replace UNC as the front-runner in collegiate women's soccer.

 WORDS TO UNDERSTAND

accolades
awards, privileges, or acknowledgments of merit

franchises
the right of membership in a professional sports league

influx
the arrival or inward flow of a large amount of something

CHAPTER 3

Going Pro

In the early to mid-1900s many women enjoyed playing soccer, but they did not do so professionally. Women's professional soccer did not yet exist in the United States, and soccer clubs did not permit women to join. The FIFA Women's World Cup and women's soccer at the Olympics would not exist until the 1990s.

PROFESSIONAL WOMEN'S SOCCER: A SLOW BUILD

In 1917, a group of female soccer players in the United Kingdom who called themselves the Dick, Kerr Ladies F.C. formed a team. There were no other women's teams for them to play against, so they played against men's teams instead. In their first season, their record was 3–2–2, which was impressive for a group of women who had never played against a men's team before. Sometimes the women on the team expressed frustration

The Dick, Kerr Ladies Football Club members pose for a group photo in 1922.

that the men's teams they played against seemed to take it easy on them. The Dick, Kerr Ladies continued to play together for the next forty-eight years, always holding themselves to a high standard and pressing the status quo when it came to women in sports.

In 1951, Father Craig of St. Matthew's Parish in St. Louis, Missouri, developed the first organized women's soccer establishment in the United States. This was different from what the Dick, Kerr Ladies organized because this consisted of multiple teams in a small league. The league continued for two seasons and consisted of four teams. Although the league did not last long, it was a huge step toward the development of a professional women's soccer organization in the United States. This was considered a club league, as the women were not paid as professional athletes. In the 1970s, women's soccer finally began to take hold at the collegiate level due to the development of Title IX. Finally, colleges and universities were required to give equal funding and access to women's sports, which resulted in the creation of many new women's varsity teams.

This growth trickled down into elementary and high schools as well, where Title IX also applies. There was a sudden **influx** of young girls interested in playing soccer. Much of the development of women's soccer in the United States started with female student-athletes. Due to long-standing traditions of male-only clubs, it took a little bit longer for women's professional soccer to become respected in the United States. Title IX applied only to educational institutions that received public funding, so while it was a huge help in getting girls involved in sports in schools, it had no effect on private clubs. Typically, scouting and talent development that leads to playing professionally happens in private clubs. Since women still did not have access to these clubs in many areas of the United States, it took a longer time for women to get their footing when it came to playing professional soccer. When looking for young players to recruit, college scouts had to go to high school games, rather than to soccer clubs where they would typically recruit male players.

Why Do Sports Matter for Girls?

Research has proven time and again that girls who play sports starting at a young age are more successful later in life. Girls who play sports in high school are 20 percent more likely to graduate from high school and 20 percent more likely to graduate from college than girls who do not play sports. There have been many components that had to come together in order to bring women's soccer to the international stage, and it starts with girls' soccer. When young girls are interested in the sport, they're more likely to play and watch, creating a new generation of soccer players and fans.

The U.S. Women's National Team was established in 1985, at a time when many European countries already had long-established national women's teams. The women were pulled from university teams, as there was not a professional soccer league established in the United States at that time. They played just one tournament that first year. The next year the women's team still played few games—a total of seven—but things began to change. In 1986, the U.S. Women's National Team's new coach was Anson Dorrance of UNC, and he brought an arsenal of knowledge to the team. Dorrance had previously coached many of the players on the 1986 team during their collegiate soccer careers. Practices and training became more professional, and Dorrance brought many star UNC players with him to join the team. Since many of the players already knew Dorrance and his approach to coaching, they were quickly able to recreate the spirit of winning that they had at UNC. Little did the team know that one day, many of them would go on to become World Cup winners and Olympic champions.

In the 1986 season, the women's team won five of their seven games and began to prove that they were a team to watch. In 1987, the team continued to improve, but they were challenged by a more difficult schedule than they had encountered in previous years. That season ended with a 6–1–4 record, which included victories against Norway and China, two of the soccer powerhouses of the time. The 1987 team included stars that had been promoted from the U-19 team including Mia Hamm, Linda Hamilton, and Kristine Lilly. The team appeared to be right around the corner from achieving international accolades, but things began to go downhill in the late 1980s. The United States teams did not have enough practice time together to become serious international contenders.

In 1991 everything changed, as the FIFA Women's World Cup was established. The inaugural event was held in China, and the U.S. women's national team (USWNT) had its first chance to show the world that it could pull together and be serious competitors on the international scene. Anson Dorrance assembled his World Cup team in April of 1991 and began putting them through practices three times each week throughout the

When Dorrance took over the USWNT in 1986, he instilled a professional approach to training and practice that quickly translated to on-field success.

summer. Dorrance realized that he had an incredible amount of talent on his hands. The team began playing internationally, and it was clear that it was a force to be reckoned with. Unlike other countries, the United States had the advantage of players who were already getting high-level training in NCAA collegiate women's soccer programs. One of the toughest teams to beat at the time was the Soviet Union (now Russia), and the USWNT beat them 8–0 in the run-up to the 1991 FIFA Women's World Cup. It was clear that the USWNT meant business.

Harvey

Werden

Biefeld

Hamm   Hamilton

Foudy

Higgins   Lilly

Heinrichs   Akers-Stahl   Jennings

Medalen

Hegstad   Riise

Carlsen   Zaborowski   Haugen

Nyborg   Svensson

Espeseth

Støre

Seth

Led by Golden Ball award–(MVP) winner Carin Jennings, the USNT defeated Norway to win the first FIFA Women's World Cup in 1991.

When the 1991 World Cup rolled around, the USWNT was the only North American team that was able to hold its own on the international stage. Only Canada was able to hold the U.S. team to less than ten goals in a game. In a qualifying game versus Mexico, U.S. defender Brandi Chastain scored five goals herself. The FIFA Women's

World Cup drew huge crowds in China, sometimes attracting more than twenty-thousand fans at a single match. The U.S. team was not used to crowds of that size, but they embraced the challenge and brought home the 1991 FIFA Women's World Cup trophy.

1
2
3
4
5 - 8
9 - 12

This map shows the order of finish for the teams in the 1995 FIFA Women's World Cup. The United States lost to eventual champions Norway in the semifinals.

In 1996 women's soccer was an Olympic event for the first time, and sports fans in the United States finally began to take notice. Coach Tony DiCicco took over for Anson Dorrance as head coach in 1994, and there was a new momentum for the team. For the first time, more attention was paid to the women's team than to the perpetually underperforming men's team. While more than seventy-six thousand fans showed up in person to watch the final women's match, the contest was not covered on national TV in the United States.

After the Olympic gold medal win, the team took another breather until getting back together in 1997 to begin gearing up for the 1999 FIFA Women's World Cup. FIFA made the decision to promote the Women's World Cup in the same way they had promoted the men's World Cup in the past, with large advertising budgets, matches held in professional stadiums, and widespread TV coverage on mainstream sports networks. While FIFA was gearing up for the tournament, the USWNT continued to get better and better. In 1997 they played eighteen matches (mostly friendlies with little tournament play), of which they won sixteen. The team continued to gear up for the World Cup with a more rigorous schedule in 1998, with a total of twenty-five matches played. Once again, the USWNT showed that they were improving even more, with a record of 22–1–2.

After scoring the tournament winning penalty kick at the 1999 FIFA Women's World Cup, Brandi Chastain burst into the most famous celebration in all of women's sports.

To this day the 1999 USWNT and its World Cup performance is still one of the most talked about groups of American athletes. The tournament brought fierce competition from Germany, Norway, and Brazil. While the United States easily beat out much of the competition in the early rounds, things began to heat up once the tournament hit the quarterfinals. Many of the matches were close, and many of the teams seemed

The gold medal match at the 2000 Olympic women's soccer tournament was held at the Sydney Football Stadium in Australia, where Norway beat the United States 3-2.

evenly matched and were playing virtually error-free soccer. An average of thirty-eight thousand fans attended each match, and the event garnered higher TV ratings in the United States than the previous men's World Cup. The final match of the 1999 FIFA Women's World Cup featured the United States. vs. China, and more than ninety-two thousand fans attended it. In an iconic final moment that came down to a penalty kick shoot-out, Chastain scored on the final penalty for the United States, clinching the victory.

Watch Brandi Chastain score the iconic game-winning goal at the 1999 FIFA Women's World Cup.

PROFESSIONAL WOMEN'S SOCCER TODAY

After the 1999 World Cup win, there was a buzz around the sport and a newly minted market for women's soccer. The Women's United States Soccer Association, or WUSA, was established. This was the first women's soccer league in the world that paid all of its players. There were eight WUSA **franchises**: Atlanta Beat, Boston Breakers, Carolina Courage, New York Power, Philadelphia Charge, San Diego Spirit, San Jose CyberRays, and Washington Freedom. While the WUSA operated for three seasons (2001 to 2003), interest was not as high as the league investors had hoped. The WUSA went on hiatus in 2003, with ultimately unrealized hopes to re-establish itself at a later date. Many of the players began to play with the Women's Premier Soccer League (a club league with over one hundred teams throughout the United States and Puerto Rico). Another league, Women's Professional Soccer (WPS) was established in 2009, but due to many of the same issues faced by WUSA, it ceased to run in 2012.

In 2018 the National Women's Soccer League (NWSL) entered its sixth season, twice as long as the professional women's leagues that came before it—WUSA and WPS. There are nine teams in the NWSL, but this number has not been consistent. Teams collapse (including the Kansas City and Boston teams), and new teams emerge (the Utah Royals started with the 2018 season) with regularity. The NWSL believes that it is poised for continued growth over the coming years for a variety of reasons. According to Amanda Duffy, NWSL managing director of operations, "The quality of our existing ownerships, the quality of our markets, quality of facilities that the teams and players have access to and each of the owners' commitment to the long-term development of this league are all areas that we feel we have right now or are in a growing position with." The NWSL believes that it has a core team of owners that are dedicated to growing the organization. As the teams, players, and facilities improve, the NWSL believes that ticket sales and viewership will improve as well.

NWSL teams like the Portland Thorns FC and Houston Dash, seen here in a match from the 2017 season, are owned and supported by MLS franchises (Portland Timbers and Houston Dynamo, respectively).

Many of the women's professional teams are paired with teams in Major League Soccer, the successful men's pro league. In some markets, this pairing increases support throughout the community. While pairing teams in no way guarantees that a franchise will be successful, it does increase the likelihood of financial success for both teams. The pairing is helpful because it provides newer women's teams with access to the men's fan base, increasing attendance for games and merchandise sales.

While Americans are always quick to support World Cup or Olympic teams every four years, women's soccer viewership takes a huge dip when a world tournament is not in the works. For example, viewership of women's professional soccer has historically risen in the year leading up to the World Cup, and then it quickly drops off after the World Cup is completed. This is slowly but surely changing in the United States, as the NWSL has been in business longer than any other women's soccer league in U.S. history. There are a number of factors that contribute to higher viewership of women's soccer, including advertising, facilities, and cost of game tickets. Many women's soccer franchise owners hope that pairing women's teams with men's teams will continue to increase viewership of women's soccer in non-World Cup years.

KEEPING MOMENTUM STRONG

There are a variety of factors that have affected the development of girls' soccer in the United States, which leads to a greater number of well-trained professional women's soccer players in the long run. Most recently, the creation of the U.S. Soccer Girls' Development Academy has opened up a new world of soccer training to young female athletes who have their sights on playing at the collegiate or professional level. Clubs that are a part of the U.S. Soccer Development Academy adhere to strict program standards (such as training at least four days each week, meaningful competition set to FIFA standards, talent identification by collegiate scouts during games, experienced referees, and travel scholarships for athletes who have financial need). U.S. Soccer Girls' Development Academy clubs are available for U-14 through U-19 girls. In order to be trained by a Development Academy club, potential players must apply and be selected during a rigorous tryout process (the specific process differs for each club). National team staff members observe every Development Academy match, giving players exposure that they are unlikely to experience in other clubs. The Development Academy also requires players to rest at least one day each week to avoid overtraining and provides players with access to advanced sports

American TV networks have embraced soccer in recent years, increasing exposure to the sport for fans old and new.

medicine and trained medical professionals at every match. Prior to 2017, the U.S. Soccer Development Academy was available only to boys. The expansion of the academy to include female athletes is likely to increase the number of female student-athletes who want to play at the collegiate level, resulting in a higher level of competition at the college level and, eventually, a higher level of competition at the professional level.

Increased airtime on mainstream sports channels has also helped to boost women's soccer viewership in the United States. In 2014 Mia Hamm stated, "I could go home right now and find four channels that have something about soccer going on, and I definitely could not have done that when I was playing." When big television networks commit to drawing in viewers to women's soccer (through promotions and advertising), reach increases. When more people are aware of women's soccer popularity builds, and more tickets are sold to live games. This type of coverage is key to helping women's soccer continue to build momentum in the United States.

GOING PRO—
OPPORTUNITIES
WORLDWIDE

One of the best things about soccer is that it's beloved throughout the world. Many professional soccer players compete in more than one country throughout their careers. In many countries—such as England, France, Spain, Brazil, and China—athletes often have access to excellent trainers and facilities on par to what they have in the United States. There is, however, a different approach to training in soccer-powerhouse countries than to the training that is typically done in the United States. For budding soccer professionals overseas, the game is top priority. The vast majority of players looking to go pro play exclusively with youth academy clubs. The main goal of these clubs is to train young players to eventually play professionally. In the United States, the focus is different. Players typically play with their high school teams and then their college teams—where an emphasis is still placed on education. In other countries, this game-first development model can, at times, provide a higher level of competition. The scholastic-development model has proven to be highly effective for American women players, however, as the USWNT is consistently FIFA's top-ranked team.

Since soccer has a larger fan base overseas than in the United States, matches have much higher attendance. Many athletes see this as a positive as they enjoy playing in front of a large crowd. While athletes may choose to play in clubs in a different country rather than in their domestic league, their national affiliation does not change.

Many soccer players choose to play professionally abroad, either because they're interested in travel, they feel that they will be able to better develop their talents in a country with more professional opportunities than their home countries, or because their home countries do not have a professional soccer league. From Australia to Italy to Germany, there are twenty-two different professional women's football leagues in the world. England's Football Association Women's Super League has been in existence since 2010, with eleven teams in the league. Norway's professional women's league, Toppserien, was founded in 1984 and consists of twelve teams throughout Norway. While many soccer fans think of European countries as the giants in the soccer world, China is not far behind. The Chinese Women's Super League (CWSL) is a professional soccer league that is growing at breakneck speed. The league started in 2007 and currently has eight clubs throughout China. Many Brazilian players choose to play for CWSL, as Brazil does not have a professional soccer league for women. The decision to play abroad is a unique choice that each athlete must make for herself. Some athletes may choose to play in a less difficult professional league in order to improve their skills to eventually be able to play for a professional league in their own countries.

2018 Champions League Cup during final match of the UEFA Women's Champions League VfL Wolfsburg—Lyon at the Valeriy Lobanovskyi Dynamo Stadium in Kyiv.

Text-Dependent Questions:

1. In what year was the U.S. Soccer Development Academy for girls created?

2. What is one reason that an American soccer player may choose to play abroad?

3. Does Title IX apply to private schools as well as public schools?

Research Project:

Two professional soccer organizations came before the National Women's Soccer League—Women's United Soccer Association and Women's Professional Soccer. Choose one of these organizations to research, and explain why the organization failed. Compare the organization you chose with the National Women's Soccer League, and explain why the NWSL has proven longer lasting than the organization you chose.

WORDS TO UNDERSTAND

EEOC
Equal Employment Opportunity Commission; a U.S. federal agency that works to ensure equal pay for all Americans who are doing equal work

incidence
the number of times something happens or develops

objectify
to treat someone as an object rather than as a person

strike
a work stoppage by a body of workers to enforce compliance with demands made on an employer

CHAPTER 4

Playing Fair

In many countries, including the United States, women's soccer simply is not treated with the same respect as men's soccer. It's taken huge strides in recent years, but there is still a long way to go. An example of this was made public in the months prior to the 2015 World Cup. Abby Wambach, a member of the USWNT, spoke publicly about her frustration that the Women's World Cup matches were played on artificial turf, while the men's matches were held on real grass. Studies have shown that there is a higher incidence of injuries on artificial turf, especially ankle injuries. Over the years, a number of members of the USWNT, including Mia Hamm, have publicly stated that they would prefer to play on real grass. Frustratingly for the women's team, the complaint was never resolved.

WOMEN'S SOCCER: THE BARRIERS

The issue of unequal treatment when compared to the men's national team continues to come up in women's soccer. In 2016, former women's national team goalie and professional soccer player Hope Solo wrote a blog post entitled, "Our Fight for Equal Pay Is about More Than Just Soccer," explaining a plethora of gender-equality issues that are often not discussed in soccer. One of Solo's key points was on the marketing that professional soccer organizations tend to use when it comes to men's and women's teams. Solo alleges that professional soccer organizations spend vastly more on promoting men's teams, and then justify their spending by saying that men's teams sell more tickets. Solo believes that this is true only because of the marketing factor, and that if all things were equal women's soccer matches would actually be more widely viewed and more highly attended than men's matches. Solo said that she believes the NWSL is more athletic and exciting to watch than the MLS. Solo went on to say that while women's soccer coverage is excellent during the World Cup and during the Olympics, the sport is rarely covered outside of those times, leading to decreased interest. She believes that if coverage were more consistent, the interest in women's soccer would grow rapidly.

Former USWNT star goalkeeper Hope Solo believes that if women's soccer received coverage outside of major tournament years, it would have rapid growth.

TITLE IX

Established in 1972, Title IX was a key step in ending the second-rate status of girls' and women's athletics. This law applies to all educational institutions that receive any public funding. All public schools, colleges, and universities (as well as the vast majority of private schools, as most receive at least some public funding) fall into this category. Under Title IX, colleges and universities must offer equal scholarship money to both male and female student-athletes in the same sport. Prior to Title IX, many schools offered larger financial aid packages to male student-athletes. The advent of Title IX created a stir among potential female student-athletes in the United States. High school girls realized that, just like their male peers, they had the opportunity to get athletic scholarships, allowing them to attend schools that they might otherwise be unable to afford. This realization drove many female student-athletes to become even better at their sport.

Title IX also applied to high school student-athletes, which in turn led to more girls being interested in playing at the collegiate level. This trickle-down effect is key in affecting change from the ground up. When more young athletes are interested in playing soccer, it forces programs to grow as the athletes grow, leading to more opportunities to play on middle school, high school, and club teams.

Outside of the United States, laws similar to Title IX unfortunately do not have a similar effect on equality in men's and women's soccer. While similar laws do exist, they apply only to educational institutions, many of which do not have the same robust athletics departments as schools in the United States. In many European countries, for example, soccer

Club soccer teams are not subject to Title IX requirements, so they can choose to spend more resources on boys' development as they see fit.

development is mainly done through club teams instead of through school teams. Educational laws do not govern private clubs, even when school-age children are playing in the clubs. This means that clubs can choose to spend more money on boys' teams than girls' teams, thus perpetuating the inequality that is seen at the professional level.

EQUAL PAY ACT

The USWNT filed a complaint with the **EEOC** in 2016. The team's claim stated that they are paid only one-fourth the amount paid to the men's national team, despite the fact that they generate more revenue than the men's team. The complaint also stated that they are paid only when they win, while the men's team is paid whether they win or lose. Both the women's national team and professional club teams have expressed complaints that hotel accommodations for women's teams are often inferior to those provided to the men's teams.

On average across the world, female professional soccer players are paid far less than men, although women's soccer programs tend to have lower operating costs (in part due to the fact that coaches of women's teams are paid less than coaches of men's teams—another problematic fact). In many countries, professional women's soccer players are paid salaries that fall below the poverty line. The USWNT negotiations with the U.S. Soccer Federation dragged on for a year, but they eventually won the following concessions, according to the *New York Times*:

- A "sizable increase" in base pay and bigger bonuses for USWNT players, which could lead to some players doubling their incomes and earning $200,000 to $300,000 per year—and even more during World Cup years

- Improved travel accommodations and working conditions—a category that likely includes field quality

- Union control over some of the USWNT licensing and marketing rights

Co-Captain Carli Lloyd was one of five USWNT players to file a complaint with the Equal Employment Opportunity Commission in 2016.

- Greater support of the National Women's Soccer League (NWSL), with a continued commitment to pay NWSL salaries for allocated USWNT players; additional field and stadium oversight; and greater bonuses for players who don't have a USWNT contract

- Per diems that are equal to the ones the men's national team receives

- More support for players who are pregnant or adopting a child

The actions of the USWNT have been a beacon for women's teams across the world and in other U.S. sports as well. For example, Norway's women's team fought for and received a pay raise that made its salary equal to that of the men's team. The U.S. women's hockey team threatened to go on **strike** and boycott the 2017 World Championship tournament, where it was the defending champion. Three days before the event, USA Hockey agreed to give the players significant pay raises and travel arrangements equal to the men's team. Equality for women's soccer has taken significant steps in recent years, but there is a long way to go.

Check out this video of the ad the USWNT players ran during their fight for equal treatment.

WOMEN'S SOCCER WORLDWIDE: THE ROADBLOCKS

In the United States and much of Europe, it's hard to imagine a society that would stop women from playing soccer. In many countries, however, this is sadly the case for many women who want to be athletes. For women in these countries, playing sports openly is a freedom for which they must fight. In Africa, Latin America, Asia, and the Middle East, many women are forbidden (either by law or by familial and cultural norms) from participating in sports. Some critics of the FIFA Women's World Cup believe that it is unfair to call it a world tournament when so many women are unable to participate. In Saudi Arabia, religious officials perpetuate the belief that it's immoral for women to participate in sports. In Egypt, male family members often forbid female relatives from playing sports, citing that it is considered forbidden in Islamic culture. In multiple Middle Eastern countries where temperatures are hot, women are still required to be covered to their wrists when they are outdoors. While they may not be technically banned from playing, it is very difficult to play in heavy clothing while temperatures are high. In many countries, strict rules about how women must dress make it difficult for them to play, and FIFA has not always been accommodating of this. Until

One of the great things about American culture is that not only are girls permitted to play sports like soccer if they choose but they are also encouraged to do so.

After the 2015 FIFA Women's World Cup, the Football Association in England tweeted that players on the women's team could go back to being "mothers, partners and daughters."

2012, FIFA prohibited women from playing professional soccer while wearing headscarves. This kept many women who wanted to play off of the field due to their religious beliefs.

Sexism in professional sports certainly exists in the Western world as well. In 2015, England's women's national team placed third in the World Cup. After their win, the U.K. Football Association tweeted that the women's team could now go back to being "mothers, partners, and daughters." While many women on the English national team are in fact mothers and spouses, the U.K. Football Association has never made a similar tweet regarding the men's team, leading many soccer fans to feel that the U.K. Football Association sees the women of the national team as mothers and wives who also play soccer, instead of soccer players who also have personal responsibilities. In Canada, women's soccer players are fighting for the right to paid maternity leave, a resource they do not currently have available.

In South America, the issue for women's professional soccer players is a little bit different. Women are encouraged to play the game (although they were not permitted to play until 1979), but they are often objectified, and their popularity is based on their appearance instead of their ability to play. The appearance of female soccer players is often used as a tactic to sell tickets to the game, instead of using their athletic ability to draw crowds. The Brazilian women's national team has expressed frustration at these advertising tactics.

In some countries, governments do not give funding to their women's national teams, or give much less funding than they give the men's national team. In 2015, Uganda's national under-twenty women's team didn't make it to the World Cup. They were trained and ready to compete, but their government pulled their funding at the last minute, and the team never got to play.

While this information is discouraging, there is proof that change is possible. Since the implementation of Title IX, the number of female athletes in the United States has risen. Today, 40 percent of all soccer players (from young players all the way to professionals) are female. Title IX has brought an entirely new generation of athletes to the soccer scene. While there is much work to be done to help level the playing field for female soccer players, the foundation is being laid and the United States is off to a good start. With FIFA's initiatives to increase the number of women involved in soccer, it's likely that even more change will happen in the coming years.

Female players in some countries, like Brazil's Érika, feel teams are marketed by emphasizing player's physical appearance rather than their skill.

WOMEN'S RIGHTS IN SOCCER: TAKING ACTION

While the treatment of women in soccer can be infuriating, many players across the world are taking action and demanding change. Spain's women's national team demanded that its male coach be fired after the players felt that they were inadequately prepared for the World Cup. After the firing of their female coach, many members of Brazil's national women's soccer team quit the team, citing that their input should have been taken into consideration before the firing of the coach. Many of Brazil's players also cited years of disrespect from the country's national soccer organization as reason for hanging up their cleats for good. In Nigeria, the national women's team held a sit-in to demand payment that they had been promised but never showed up in their bank accounts. The team alleged that the Nigerian government owed each player more than seventeen thousand dollars. The players stated that they felt like they were being treated as children, rather than as professional athletes. The team was told that the funds were not available to pay them, but they believed this to be untrue, as the men's team continued to receive salaries.

Some women's national teams have turned to striking in order to show their national soccer federations that they are serious about their demands. Ireland's national team threatened to strike, citing the fact that they were treated like "fifth-rate citizens." The team stated that they were expected to share warm-up suits, were not given proper locker rooms in which to change before games (they had to change in the bathrooms of airports prior to their games),

The Nigerian women's soccer team protested because while its bonuses were withheld due to an alleged lack of funds, the country's men's team continued to be paid.

and that they were not given gym memberships. All of these grievances are unheard of for men's teams. The Australian women's national team actually did go on strike following a successful 2015 FIFA Women's World Cup. They stopped getting paid, and many of the players had to take on other jobs in order to make ends meet. They asked for a salary increase (to a modest twenty-eight thousand dollars per year), as well as better accommodations and monetary bonuses for playing international matches. The team eventually came to an agreement with Football Federation Australia and returned to the playing field.

Speaking out against national soccer federations on the grounds of gender inequality can be scary for players. Some players fear that they could lose their contracts and, with those contracts, their professional careers. Many players are so grateful to be playing at the professional level that they fear making waves with their sport's governing body. It's important that women continue to fight and demand equal treatment in sports.

Equality on the Field

FIFA is studying gender equality issues in soccer in an effort to understand, and then change, these issues for the better. At a 2015 FIFA symposium, female delegates from 171 countries were surveyed on gender discrimination in soccer. Sixty-three percent of the women surveyed said that they had witnessed gender discrimination in soccer, either at the management level or on the field. Forty-three percent of these women said that they had experienced gender discrimination in soccer themselves. Eighty-two percent of women surveyed said that they believed that gender discrimination was stopping women's soccer from realizing its full potential worldwide.

FIFA has been progressive in recent years in addressing the issue of gender inequality within the organization.

FIFA readily admits that gender discrimination is a problem in soccer, and it is taking a number of steps to change that. While FIFA has not always been an ally to female soccer players, that is quickly changing. In 2015 FIFA released a report on women in soccer and cited a number of areas that need improvement, including the need for higher funding, the benefits of increasing the number of women's soccer matches and licensed players, and the need for a highesr number of female coaches (currently, only 7 percent of professional soccer coaches are female). By discontinuing their ban on head coverings in 2012, FIFA showed a growing respect for women of all cultures engaging in soccer.

Text-Dependent Questions:

1. Name three national teams that have taken a stand and demanded better treatment for women in soccer.

2. Why do many teams look to the Norway women's team as the ultimate example of gender equality in women's soccer?

3. What is Title IX?

Research Project:

In most countries, women's soccer players are paid less than their male counterparts. Research the pay levels for the top women's soccer players and the top men's soccer players in five different countries. Which country from those you researched has the largest pay gap between male and female soccer players? Research potential reasons behind why the gap is so large.

 WORDS TO UNDERSTAND

reform
to put or change something into an improved state or condition

representation
when someone speaks or acts on behalf of someone else

restructure
to change the makeup, organization, or pattern of something

CHAPTER 5

Changes at the Top

FIFA has recognized the fact that women's soccer faces challenges that are different from men's soccer, and in 2016, **reforms** were put into place to help women continue to be recognized as athletes that are just as entertaining, athletic, and talented as their male counterparts. It's clear that change has to start at the top, and FIFA is committed to making this happen. FIFA is working to increase viewership of soccer worldwide, and the organization realizes that it's imperative to focus specifically on women's soccer in order to maximize viewership and widen fan bases.

LOOKING FORWARD: FIFA 2.0

Caroline Gianni Infantino, the president of FIFA, has a three-part plan to improve FIFA as an organization. First, Infantino wants to invest in soccer and its players, which of course includes women players and teams. Next, he wants to improve the soccer experience for fans. Lastly, he wants to bring more women to the management level within FIFA. Infantino recognizes that he cannot move the world of women's soccer forward without women's input in leadership-level decisions. This is a change from the management style FIFA has held previously, with men making nearly all of the important decisions about women's soccer. Women's **representation** is a key piece of FIFA 2.0.

FIFA has implemented a plan to invest heavily in soccer and its players, especially the women's game.

Currently 45 percent of the world's population is involved with soccer in some way—as a player, fan, referee, or coach. Infantino wants to raise this number to 60 percent, which means that outreach to female fans and players must become a priority. This is just the first step in helping women's soccer to become more mainstream. FIFA has a goal of having sixty million female soccer players worldwide by 2026—this is double the current number. As more girls are encouraged to participate in soccer, collegiate soccer will become more competitive, which will lead to more exciting, competitive, and athletic matches. This change

FIFA President Gianni Infantino has implemented a three-part plan to improve the sport's governing body.

is likely to lead in turn to increasingly competitive professional women's soccer matches and World Cup tournaments. As mentioned previously, it's imperative that this change take place from the ground up, starting with getting young girls interested in soccer and offering them the opportunity to play at an early age. It's key that FIFA starts this **restructuring** from the ground up organizationally as well, bringing on female skill-development coaches (specifically at the grassroots level, in areas where organized soccer is in the beginning stages) as well as higher-level leadership. While bringing in older fans is a big help in increasing viewership, the only way to create sustainable, long-lasting change is to get girls interested in playing and watching soccer at a young age.

In 2016, FIFA realized that it needed to have a group of leaders specifically dedicated to growing women's soccer, and for that it created the Women's Football Division, with former soccer player Sarai Bareman of New Zealand as the Chief Women's Football Officer. Bareman played for the Samoan national team and previously worked as the chief executive officer of the Samoan Football Organization. Her experience in finance and business, as well as her soccer expertise, made her a great fit for the position. While it may seem obvious that a woman would be best to lead the Women's Football Division, this appointment was a surprise to many, as FIFA leadership has been historically male.

FIFA's Chief Women's Football Officer Sarai Bareman receiving an iconic present awarded to her for the inspection of potential stadiums for the 2018 FIFA U17 Women's World Cup.

FIFA is changing the women's tournaments as well. In 2018, Infantino put forth a request to the FIFA executive committee for the development of a new worldwide women's league. If approved, this competition would feature sixteen top-level women's soccer teams, and play could begin as soon as November 2019. The proposed plan also includes the development of four regional leagues across the world. Players in these regional leagues could then be scouted and offered contracts in the professional leagues, much like the minor to major league baseball system currently established in the United States. This plan is in line with Infantino's goal of increasing the number of female soccer players worldwide. The league would have a championship similar to the style of the World Cup, in hopes that this would increase the fan base and viewership of women's soccer as a whole.

Part of FIFA's future plans is a top-level, worldwide women's league.

WOMEN IN CHARGE

Women account for 8% of the total number of executive committee and board members recorded in a 2014 FIFA survey. The highest percentage was observed in the OFC* (15%), while the lowest percentage was observed in CONMEBOL (2%). This finding highlights the difficulties facing women in reaching senior positions in soccer's governing bodies.

* - inside CONCACAF, Canada and the United States are at 19%

FATMA SAMBA DIOUF SAMOURA

Position: Secretary General, FIFA

Country: Senegal

DOB: 9/9/1962

› Appointed 2016
› 2nd highest ranking official in FIFA
› Runs FIFA's $5 billion commercial and operations business

LYDIA NSEKERA

Position: FIFA Council Member

Country: Burundi

DOB: 4/20/1967

› Elected 2013
› First woman ever elected to the FIFA Executive Committee
› Member of the International Olympic Committee

	Av. Number of Representatives on Executive Committees per MA	% of Women on Executive Committees
AFC	14	9%
CAF	13	8%
CONCACAF	11	13%
USA-CAN	16	19%
CONMEBOL	19	2%
OFC	8	15%
UEFA	15	6%

FLORENCE HARDOUIN

Position: Director General, French
Football Federation

Country: France

DOB: 9/9/1962

> Appointed 2013

> First woman elected to the UEFA
Executive Committee in 2016

> Former international fencing
champion

MARINA GRANOVSKAIA

Position: Director, Chelsea
Football Club

Country: Russia

DOB: 1/13/1975

> Chelsea FC board member
since 2013

> Handles player transactions for
the $1.85 billion club

> Fluent in several languages,
she is a dual citizen of
Russia and Canada

Why Does Gender Discrimination Exist in FIFA?

This is a tricky issue—technically, gender discrimination was never permitted in FIFA. The association had a culture of discrimination that allowed certain behaviors to go unreported, and this resulted in women not being treated fairly. FIFA recognizes this and realizes that reform must happen in order to give women a fair shot both in the business of soccer and on the field.

By late 2019, FIFA plans to have four regional professional women's leagues running across the globe.

FIFA 2.0—ACTION STEPS

Like most things in the professional sports world, there is little that can be done without increasing funds, and FIFA is doing just that. From 2016 to 2026, FIFA has committed to spending $315 million on women's soccer. This money will go to FIFA clubs worldwide to invest in the development of women's and girls' soccer. It will be spent in a variety of ways, including the creation and organization of girls' leagues, the improvement of already existing girls' leagues, organizing new women's professional leagues, and studying the best ways to increase the popularity of women's soccer worldwide. Bareman was a part of the 2016 FIFA Reform Committee, where she advocated for change within the organization. Bareman believed that FIFA needed to establish standards for holding women in leadership positions, and the rest of the Reform Committee unanimously agreed.

FIFA recognizes that these changes will take time and that it will be a process to usher women into leadership roles in its previously male-dominated organization. In order to move the process

FIFA's new development program is focused on getting former female players, like Pia Sundhage, involved in player development. Sundhage had 146 caps for Sweden and went on to coach both the USWNT and the Swedish national women's team.

Watch how the FIFA Women's World Cup has changed over time, and see what could be underway for the 2019 women's tournament.

along, FIFA has launched a female leadership development program for women who hope to become leaders in soccer. FIFA has recognized that if it wants to increase viewership and have a higher number of female soccer players worldwide it must first establish strong female leaders within the organization who can advocate for and understand the needs of female soccer players. The development program is also focused on encouraging former professional women's soccer players to step out of retirement and into development roles at FIFA. To that end, thirty-five women were accepted into the development program in 2015. The program consists of three leadership development modules and lasts for a total of nine months. Admission to the program is competitive, and all participants must complete a project that has the potential to transform women's soccer worldwide. Participants are paired with experienced mentors who can give them a unique perspective into soccer leadership.

FIFA has committed to making sure that female players, coaches, and leaders have a clear pathway to their desired destinations in the soccer world. The organization recognizes that many talented women have been stopped from achieving their athletic and professional goals due to harassment, unfair standards, and an unwelcoming environment. FIFA also has admitted that it realizes the need to take time to rebuild trust with female players and fans. With these new initiatives in place, FIFA hopes to level the playing field to allow women's soccer to shine.

FIFA 2.0—WHAT DOES IT MEAN FOR WOMEN'S SOCCER?

FIFA believes that having more women involved at soccer's highest levels will have a positive effect for female players at all levels.

From increasing women's pay to better playing and training facilities, it stands to reason that the FIFA reforms it will have a number of impacts on women's soccer. As women begin to enter the leadership ranks at FIFA, more advocacy will happen for female players and coaches. It's difficult to say exactly what will change first, but as more women are making leadership decisions things will change in a positive way for women's soccer players. It's likely that the salaries of women's soccer teams will increase, and it's also likely that the facilities in which they play will improve.

Text-Dependent Questions:

1. What percentage of the world's women are involved in soccer in some way?

2. What amount of money has FIFA committed to spend to develop women's soccer by the year 2026?

3. If Infantino's proposed new worldwide soccer league is created, when will play begin?

Research Project:

Research FIFA's female leadership development program. What are some of the skills that women learn while attending this program? Could you ever see yourself attending this program? Explain why or why not in a two-page report.

Club: collective name for a team, and the organization that runs it.

CONCACAF: acronym for the *Confederation of North, Central American and Caribbean Association Football*, the governing body of the sport in North and Central America and the Caribbean; pronounced "kon-ka-kaff".

Extra time: additional period, normally two halves of 15 minutes, used to determine the winner in some tied cup matches.

Full-time: the end of the game, signaled by the referees whistle (also known as the *final whistle*).

Goal difference: net difference between goals scored and goals conceded. Used to differentiate league or group stage positions when clubs are tied on points.

Hat trick: when a player scores three goals in a single match.

Own goal: where a player scores a goal against her own team, usually as the result of an error.

Penalty area: rectangular area measuring 44 yards (40.2 meters) by 18 yards (16.5 meters) in front of each goal; commonly called "the box".

Penalty kick: kick taken 12 yards (11 meters) from goal, awarded when a team commits a foul inside its own penalty area.

Penalty shootout: method of deciding a match in a knockout competition, which has ended in a draw after full-time and extra-time. Players from each side take turns to attempt to score a penalty kick against the opposition goalkeeper. Sudden death is introduced if scores are level after each side has taken five penalties.

Side: Another word for team

Stoppage time: an additional number of minutes at the end of each half, determined by the match officials, to compensate for time lost during the game. Informally known by various names, including *injury time* and *added time*.

UEFA: acronym for *Union of European Football Associations*, the governing body of the sport in Europe; pronounced "you-eh-fa".

Downing, Erin. *For Soccer-Crazy Girls Only: Everything Great about Soccer.* New York City: Feiwel & Friends, 2014.

Hamm, Mia. *Go for the Goal: A Champion's Guide to Winning in Soccer and Life.* New York: It Books, 2000.

Lisi, Clemente A. *The U.S. Women's Soccer Team.* Lexington, MA: Taylor Trade Publishing, 2013.

Lloyd, Carli. *When Nobody Was Watching: My Hard-Fought Journey to the Top of the Soccer World.* Wilmington, DE: Mariner Books, 2017.

Morgan, Alex. *Breakaway: Beyond The Goal.* New York City: Simon & Schuster Books For Young Readers, 2017.

INTERNET RESOURCES

https://www.fifa.com/womensworldcup/index.htm
Stay updated on the latest news surrounding the Women's World Cup!

https://goheels.com/index.aspx?path=wsoc
Check out the latest roster, read stories on your favorite UNC women's soccer players, and see the schedule for the upcoming season.

https://www.ncaa.com/sports/soccer-women/d1
Learn more about Division I schools and players, as well as what it takes to become a student-athlete at a Division I school.

http://www.nwslsoccer.com
Check match schedules, statistics on your favorite players, and watch videos of the latest updates in women's soccer.

https://www.ussoccer.com/womens-national-team#tab-1
Check out biographies and videos of your favorite U.S. women's team players, along with current schedules and stories on how the players of the USWNT got to where they are today.

INDEX

Abroad, U.S. players, 47
Arizona State, 25
Association for Intercollegiate Athletics for Women (AIAW), 31
Atlantic Coast Conference, 30, 32
Australia, 61
AYSO, 9–10

Ban on women's soccer, 8–9, 57
Bareman, Sarai, 68, 73
Brazil, 41, 48, 59–60
Byers, Mike, 30

Canada, 12
Castleton State College, 21–22
Chastain, Brandi, 16, 39, 41–42
China, 42
Chinese Women's Super League (CWSL), 48
Cobey, Bill, 30
College soccer, 21–33
    first team, 21–22
    funding, 22
    programs, 23–24
    recognized, 22
Cost of soccer, 11
Craig, Father, 36

DiCicco, Tony, 40
Dick, Kerr Ladies Football Club, 35–36
Dorrance, Anson, 30–31, 37–38, 40
Duffy, Amanda, 43
Duke University, 25

Education Amendments of 1972, 22–23
England's Football Association Women's Super League, 48, 58
Equal Employment Opportunity Commission (EEOC), 54–55
Érika, 60

FIFA improvements, 65–75
    development roles, 74
    executive committee and board members, 70
    for fans, 65
    funding, 73
    girls' leagues, 73
    investments, 65
    leadership, 70–71, 73–74
    new women's league, 68
    restructuring, 67
    viewership, 74
    women in management, 65
FIFA Women's World Cup, 15, 35, 38, 57, 74
    1991, 39
    1995, 40
    1999, 16, 40–42
    2015, 61
    2017, 58
FIFA Women's World Player of the Year, 33
Football Federation Australia, 61
Funding for teams, 59

Gender equality, 19, 21–23, 36, 51–54, 56–57, 59, 62–63, 72
Germany, 41
Goals for Girls, 16
Granovskaia, Marina, 70
Grass vs.. turf, 51

Hamilton, Linda, 38
Hamm, Mia, 16, 19, 32–33, 38, 46, 51
Hardouin, Florence, 70
Harper's Bazaar, 7
Headscarves, 57, 59
Heath, Tobin, 33
High school soccer, 12–13

Infantino, Gianni, 65, 67–68
Involvement in soccer, 67
Ireland, 61
Islam, 57

Jennings, Carin, 39

Kerr, Sam, 24
Klingenberg, Meghan, 32
Korbus, Joe, 10

Lilly, Kristine, 33, 38
Lloyd, Carli, 55

Maehabo, Mario, 10
Major League Soccer (MLS), 16, 44
Marketing, 52

Mexico, 39
Meyers, Ann, 23

National Professional Soccer League (NPSL), 9
NCAA Division I, 21–25
    admission, 26
    cost of education, 27
    getting into, 28
    likelihood of professional contract, 28
    scholarships, 26–28
    schools, 25
New York Times, 54
Nigeria, 60–61
North American Soccer League (NASL), 9, 15
Norway, 39, 41, 48, 56
Nsekera, Lydia, 70

Objectification of women, 59
Olympic Games
    1996, 40
    2000, 42
Open registration, 10

Parlow, Cindy, 33
Penn State University, 25
Popularity of girls' soccer, 11
Professional soccer, 35–48

Reforms, 65–75
Resurgence of women's soccer, 9
Rickleffs, Ron, 10
Rights for women's soccer players, 60–63
Roadblocks, 57–63

Salaries, 54, 61
Samoan Football Organization, 68
Samoura, Fatma Samba Diouf, 70
Senior players, 13
Solo, Hope, 51–52
Soviet Union, 38
Spain, 60
St. Matthew's Parish, St. Louis, 36
Stanford, 32
Strikes, 61
Sundhage, Pia, 73

Title IX, 22–23, 36, 52–54
    elementary and high school, 36, 53
    and rise of female athletes, 59–60

scholarships, 52–53
Toppserien, 48
Tryouts, 10
TV and soccer, 15–16

UEFA Women's Champions League, 48
Uganda, 59
U.K. Football Association, 59
United Kingdom, 29
University of North Carolina at Chapel Hill Tar Heels, 22, 25, 29–33
    Atlantic Coast Conference Championships (ACC), 30, 32
    dominance of, 31
    McCaskill Soccer Center, 29
    NCAA Division I Women's Soccer Championships, 30, 32
U.S. National Women's Soccer League (NWSL), 43, 56
U.S. Soccer Federation, 54
U.S. Soccer Girls' Development Academy, 45–46
U.S. Women's National Team (USWNT), 17–19, 37–41, 54, 56
U.S. Women's Soccer Team, 7
U.S. Women's World Cup Team, 14
U.S. Youth Soccer, 10
Utah State, 25

Venturini, Tisha, 33
Viewership of women's soccer, 45–46

Wambach, Abby, 51
Women involvement in soccer, beginnings, 7–8
Women's Football Division, 68
Women's Premier Soccer League, 43
Women's United States Soccer Association (WUSA), 43
World Cup
    1994, 16
Worldwide opportunities for soccer, 47–48

Youth soccer, 7–8, 10, 36
    benefits of, 15, 37
    cost, 16
    participation rates, 14

AUTHOR'S BIOGRAPHY

Elizabeth Roseborough is a former teacher and track coach currently living in Dayton, OH. When she's not writing, Elizabeth enjoys weight lifting, running, playing sports, and traveling with her husband, son, and dog.

EDUCATIONAL VIDEO LINKS

Chapter 1: http://x-qr.net/1DKo
Chapter 2: http://x-qr.net/1GrQ
Chapter 3: http://x-qr.net/1F5M

Chapter 4: http://x-qr.net/1Fvt
Chapter 5: http://x-qr.net/1DtM

PICTURE CREDITS